4 CHORD WORSHIP SONGS
FOR GUITAR

ISBN 978-1-4234-9644-1

HAL•LEONARD®
CORPORATION
7777 W. BLUEMOUND RD. P.O. BOX 13819 MILWAUKEE, WI 53213

Visit Hal Leonard Online at
www.halleonard.com

All the Earth Will Sing Your Praises

Words and Music by Paul Baloche

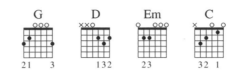

Verse
Moderately fast

You took, You take our sins a-way, O ___ God. ___

___ You give, You gave Your

life a-way for ___ us. ___ You came down,

You saved us through the ___ cross. ___

Our hearts are changed be-cause of Your great ___ love. ___

Chorus

___ You lived, You died,

You said in three days You would rise; _____ You did.

You're a - live. _____

You rule, You reign, You said You're

com - ing back a - gain. _____ I know You will, and

all the earth will sing Your prais - es, _____

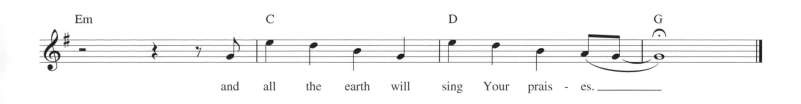

and all the earth will sing Your prais - es. _____

All We Need

Words and Music by Charlie Hall

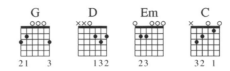

Chorus
Moderately fast

And we _____ have all _____ we need _____ in You, _____

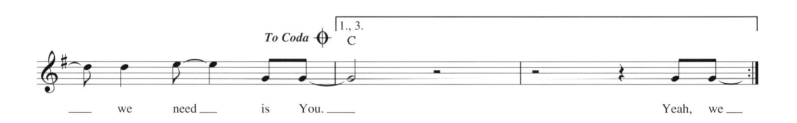

_____ and all _____ we need _____ is You, _____ all _____

_____ we need _____ is You. _____ Yeah, we _____

_____ Rich or poor, God, _____

_____ I want _____ You more _____ than an - y - thing that glit - ters in _____ this world.

_____ Be my all, all - con - sum - ing fire. _____

And You can have all my hands can hold, my heart, mind

and strength and soul. Be my all, all - con - sum - ing fire.

D.S. al Coda *(with repeat)* ⨁ **Coda**

'Cause we All we need,

Outro

all we need,

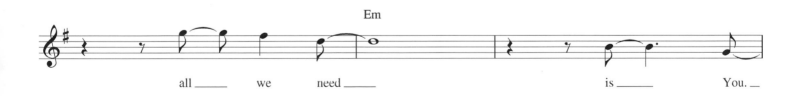

all we need is You.

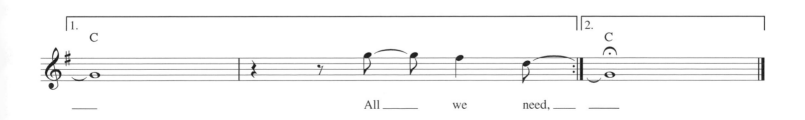

All we need,

Ancient Words

Words and Music by Lynn DeShazo

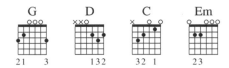

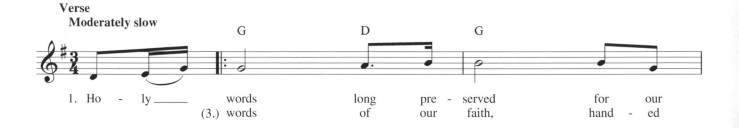

Verse
Moderately slow

1. Ho - ly _____ words long pre - served for our
(3.) words of our faith, hand - ed

walk in this world, they re - sound with God's own
down to this age, came to _____ us through sac - ri -

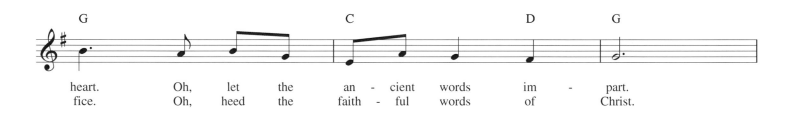

heart. Oh, let the an - cient words im - part.
fice. Oh, heed the faith - ful words of Christ.

Verse

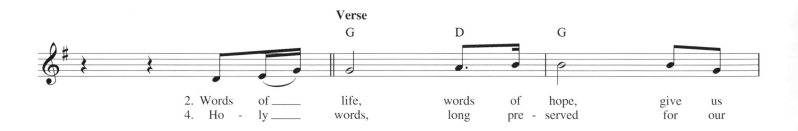

2. Words of _____ life, words of hope, give us
4. Ho - ly _____ words, long pre - served for our

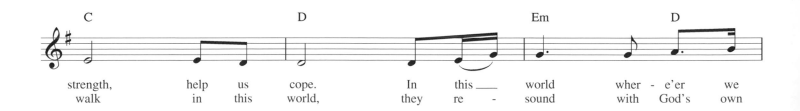

strength, help us cope. In this _____ world wher - e'er we
walk in this world, they re - sound with God's own

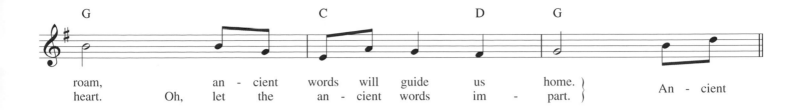

roam, an - cient words will guide us home. }
heart. Oh, let the an - cient words im - part. }
An - cient

𝄋 Chorus

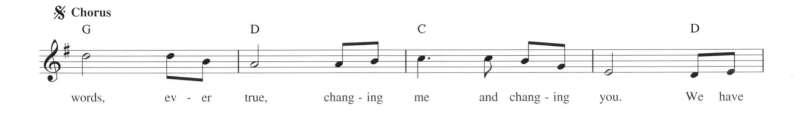

words, ev - er true, chang - ing me and chang - ing you. We have

To Coda ⊕

come with o - pen hearts. Oh, let the an - cient words im -

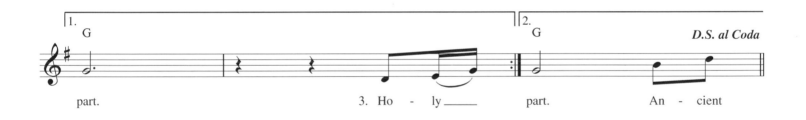

1.
part.
3. Ho - ly____ part.

2.
D.S. al Coda
An - cient

⊕ **Coda**

Tag (Slower)

part. We have come with o - pen

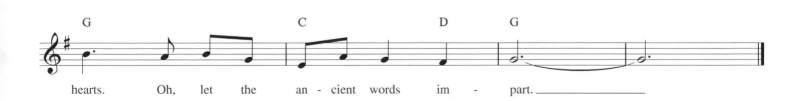

hearts. Oh, let the an - cient words im - part.____

Awesome God

Words and Music by Rich Mullins

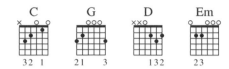

Chorus
Moderately

Our God is an awe-some God; He reigns from _ heav-en a-bove with

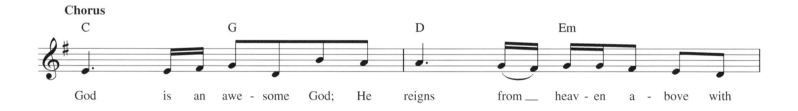

wis-dom, _ pow'r and love. Our God is an awe-some God! Our

Chorus

God is an awe-some God; He reigns from _ heav-en a-bove with

wis-dom, _ pow'r and love. Our God is an awe-some God! Our

Tag

God is an awe-some God! Our God is an awe-some God!

Breathe

Words and Music by Marie Barnett

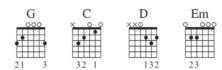

Verse
Moderately slow

This is __ the air __ I breathe, __ this is __ the air __

__ I breathe, __ Your ho - ly pres - ence liv - ing in me. __

This is __ my dai - ly bread, __ this is __ my dai -

- ly bread, __ Your ver - y Word _____

Chorus

spo - ken to me. _____ And I, _____

__ I'm des - p'rate for __ You. __ And I, _____

__ I'm lost with - out __ You. __

Awesome Is the Lord Most High

Words and Music by Chris Tomlin, Jesse Reeves, Cary Pierce and Jon Abel

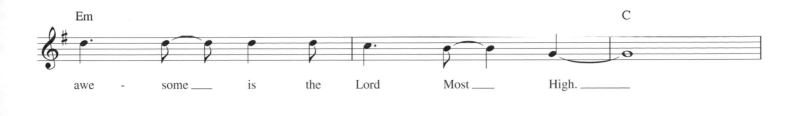

awe - some ___ is the Lord Most ___ High. ___

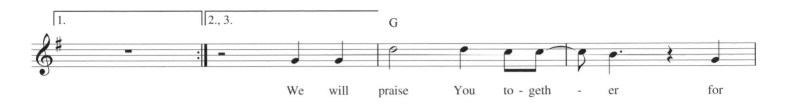

We will praise You to-geth - er for

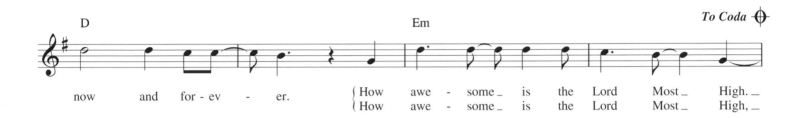

now and for-ev - er. How awe - some _ is the Lord Most _ High. _
How awe - some _ is the Lord Most _ High, _

Bridge

___ Hal - le - lu - jah,

hal - le - lu - jah, how awe - some ___ is the

Lord Most ___ High. ___ Raise your

✛ **Coda**

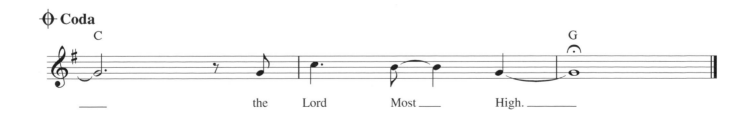

___ the Lord Most ___ High. ___

Forever

Words and Music by Chris Tomlin

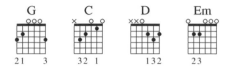

Verse
Moderately fast

1. Give thanks to the Lord, ___ our God and ___ King. ___ His
2. With a might - y hand and out - stretched ___ arm, ___ His
3. From the ris - ing to the set - ting ___ sun, ___ His

love en - dures ___ for - ev - er.
love en - dures ___ for - ev - er.
love en - dures ___ for - ev - er. And by the

For He is good, ___ He is a - bove all ___ things. ___ His
For the life ___ that's been re - born, ___ His
grace of ___ God ___ we will car - ry ___ on. ___ His

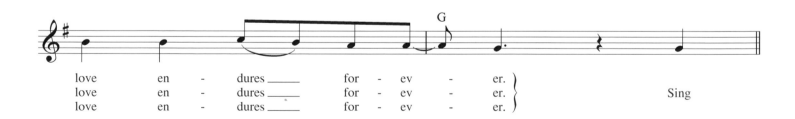

love en - dures ___ for - ev - er.   Sing
love en - dures ___ for - ev - er.
love en - dures ___ for - ev - er.

Pre-Chorus

praise, _____   sing praise. _____

Sing praise,_____ sing praise._____

Chorus

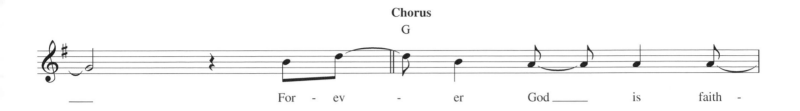

For - ev - er God_____ is faith -

- ful, for - ev - er God_____ is strong,_____

____ for - ev - er God_____ is with_____

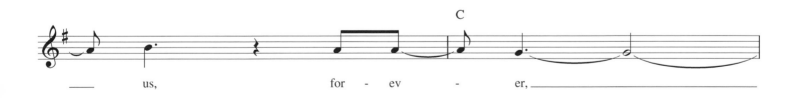

____ us, for - ev - er,_____

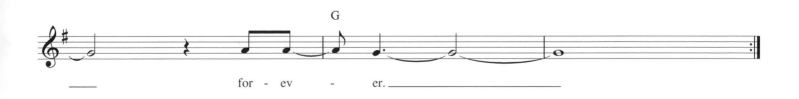

____ for - ev - er._____

Give Us Clean Hands

Words and Music by Charlie Hall

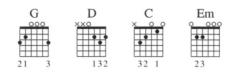

We bow our hearts,   we bend our knees.   O Spir - it, come make us hum-

ble.   We turn our eyes   from e - vil things.

O Lord, we cast down our i - dols.   Give us clean __ hands, __

give us pure __ hearts. __   Let us not __ lift our souls __ to an - oth-

- er.   Give us clean __ hands, ____   give us pure __ hearts. __

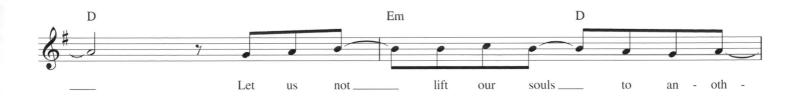

Let us not _____ lift our souls _____ to an - oth -

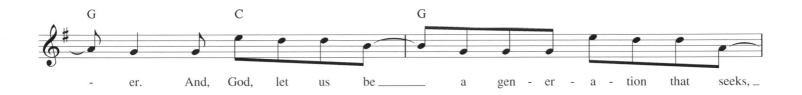

- er. And, God, let us be _____ a gen - er - a - tion that seeks, _

_____ that seeks Your face, _____ O _____ God _____ of Ja -

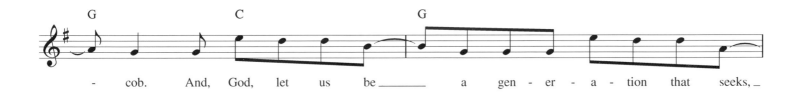

- cob. And, God, let us be _____ a gen - er - a - tion that seeks, _

_____ that seeks Your face, _____ O _____ God _____ of Ja -

- cob. _____

Glory to God Forever

Words and Music by Steve Fee and Vicky Beeching

Everyday

Words and Music by Joel Houston

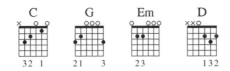

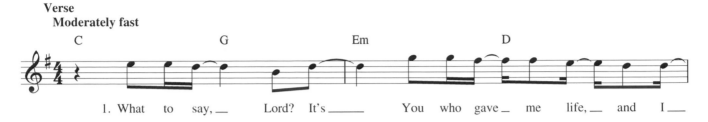

Verse
Moderately fast

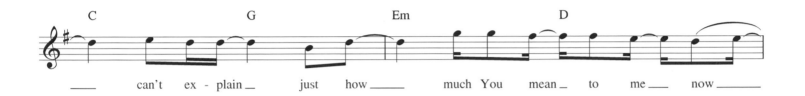

1. What to say, __ Lord? It's ___ You who gave __ me life, __ and I __

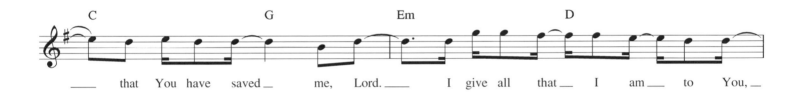

__ can't ex - plain __ just how ___ much You mean __ to me __ now ___

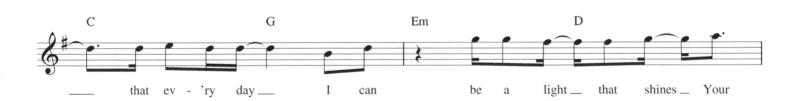

__ that You have saved __ me, Lord. ___ I give all that __ I am __ to You, __

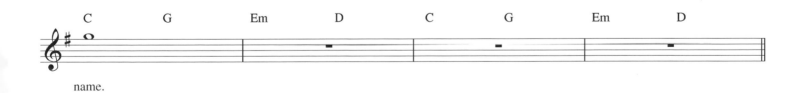

__ that ev - 'ry day __ I can be a light __ that shines __ Your

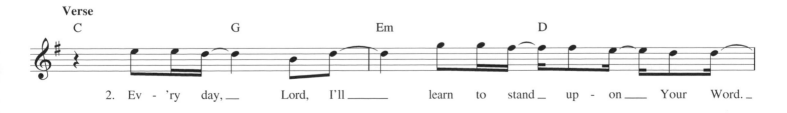

name.

Verse

2. Ev - 'ry day, __ Lord, I'll ___ learn to stand __ up - on ___ Your Word. __

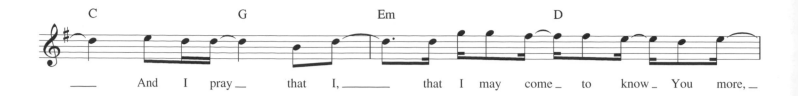

C   G   Em   D

____ And I pray ___ that I, _____ that I may come ___ to know ___ You more, ___

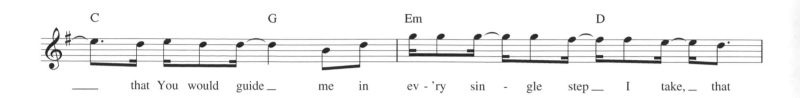

C   G   Em   D

____ that You would guide ___ me in ev - 'ry sin - gle step ___ I take, ___ that

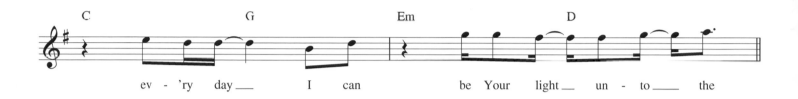

C   G   Em   D

ev - 'ry day ___ I can be Your light ___ un - to ___ the

𝄉 Chorus

G   C   Em   D

(world.) Ev - 'ry day, ___ it's You I'll live for. _____

G   C   Em   D   G   C

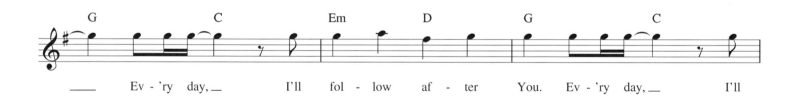

___ Ev - 'ry day, ___ I'll fol - low af - ter You. Ev - 'ry day, ___ I'll

Em   D   G   C   Em   D

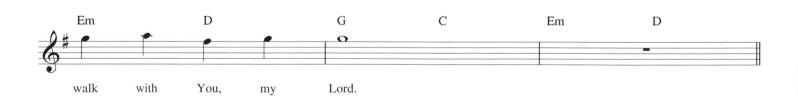

walk with You, my Lord.

Chorus

G   C   Em   D   G   C

Ev - 'ry day, ___ it's You I'll live for. _____ Ev - 'ry day, ___ I'll

fol - low af - ter You. Ev - 'ry day, __ I'll walk with You, my

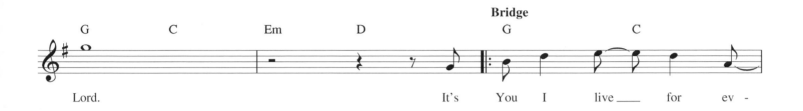

Lord. **Bridge** It's You I live __ for ev -

- 'ry day. _____ It's You I live _____ for ev -

- 'ry day. __ It's You I live __ for ev - 'ry day. _____

1. 2. *D.S. al Coda*

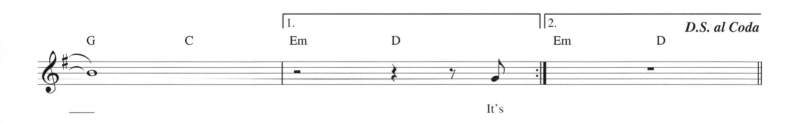

_____ It's

Coda

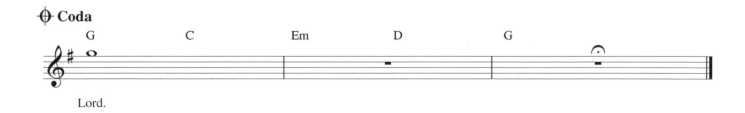

Lord.

Grace Flows Down

Words and Music by Louie Giglio, David Bell and Rod Padgett

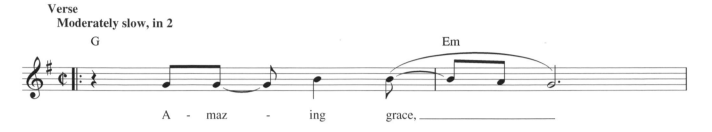

Verse
Moderately slow, in 2

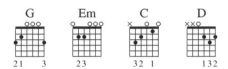

A - maz - ing grace, _____

how sweet ___ the sound; ___ a - maz - ing love, _

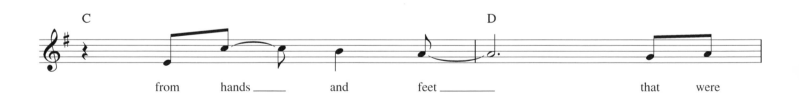

_____ now flow - ing down _____

C

from hands _____ and feet _____ that were

G

nailed _____ to _____ the tree, _____

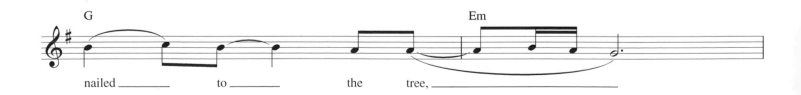

as grace ___ flows down ___ and cov - ers me. ___

Chorus

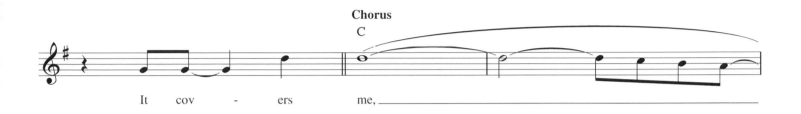

It cov - ers me, ___

___ it cov - ers me, ___

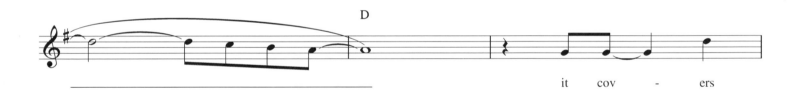

it cov - ers

me, ___ and cov - ers

me. ___

Hosanna
(Praise Is Rising)

Words and Music by Paul Baloche and Brenton Brown

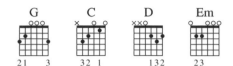

Verse
Moderately fast

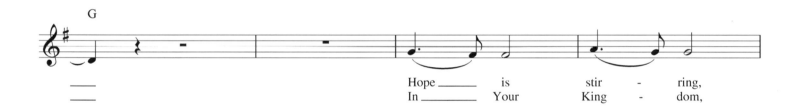

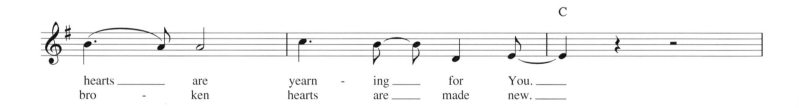

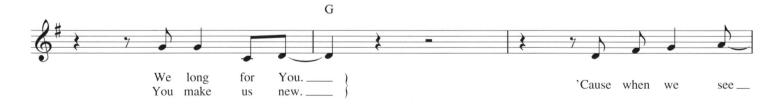

In Your pres - ence, all our fears ___ are washed a - way,

Chorus

washed a - way. ___ Ho - san -

na, ho - san - na. ___ You are the God ___

___ who saves us, ___ wor - thy of all ___ our prais - es. ___

___ Ho - san - na, ho - san - na. ___

___ Come have Your way ___ a - mong us. ___ We wel - come You here, ___

___ Lord Je - sus. ___

How Great Is Our God

Words and Music by Chris Tomlin, Jesse Reeves and Ed Cash

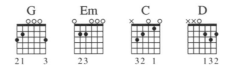

Verse
Moderately slow

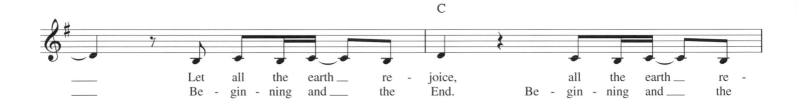

1. The splen-dor of ___ a King, ___ clothed in maj-es-ty. ___
(2.) age to age ___ He stands, ___ and time is in ___ His hands. ___

Let all the earth ___ re-joice, all the earth ___ re-
Be-gin-ning and ___ the End. Be-gin-ning and ___ the

joice. He wraps ___ Him-self ___ in light, ___ and
End. The God-head, Three ___ in One, ___

dark-ness tries ___ to hide. ___ It trem-bles at ___ His
Fa-ther, Spir-it, Son, ___ the Li-on and ___ the

Chorus

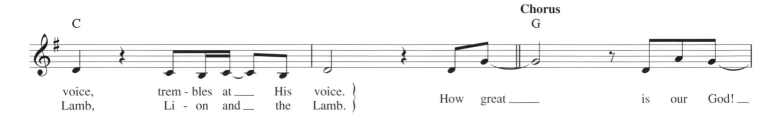

voice, trem-bles at ___ His voice. } How great ___ is our God! ___
Lamb, Li-on and ___ the Lamb. }

___ Sing with me, ___ how great is our God! And all ___ will see how

great,   how great &underline{   } is our God! &underline{ }   2. And

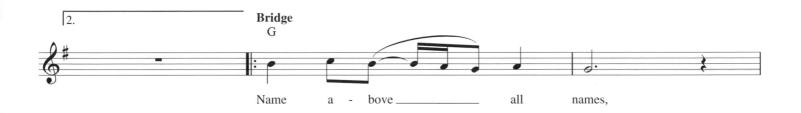

Name a - bove &underline{   } all names,

wor - thy of &underline{   } all praise.   My heart will sing, &underline{ } "How great &underline{ }

&underline{ } is our God!" &underline{ }   How great &underline{ }

&underline{ } is our God! &underline{ }   Sing with me, &underline{ } how great   is our God! &underline{ }

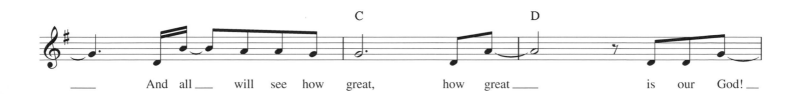

&underline{ } And all &underline{ } will see how great,   how great &underline{ } is our God! &underline{ }

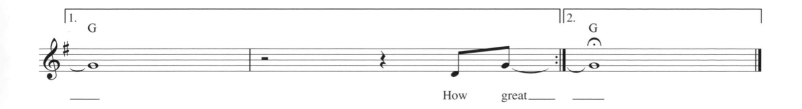

&underline{ }   How great &underline{ } &underline{ }

I Want to Know You
(In the Secret)

Words and Music by Andy Park

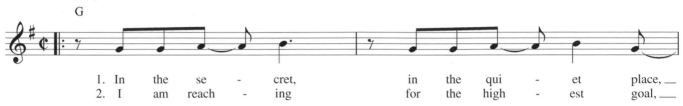

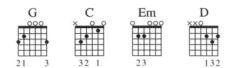

Verse
Moderately slow, in 2

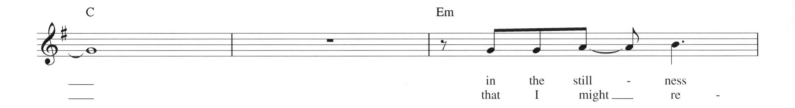

1. In the se - cret, in the qui - et place, ___
2. I am reach - ing for the high - est goal, ___

___ in the still - ness
___ that I might ___ re -

You are there. _____ In the se - cret,
ceive the prize. _____ Press - ing on - ward,

in the qui - et ho - ur I wait ___ on - ly for You, ___ }
push - ing ev - 'ry hin - drance a - side, ___ out ___ of my way, ___ }

'cause I want ___ to know You more. _____

% **Chorus**

I want to know You, ___ I want to

hear Your ___ voice. I want to know You ___ more. ___

I want to

touch You, ___ I want to see Your ___ face.

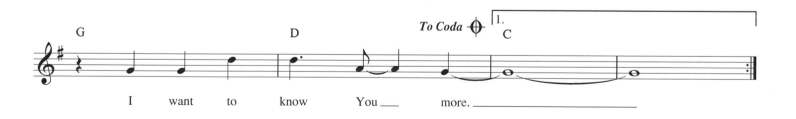

To Coda ⊕ |1.

I want to know You ___ more. ___

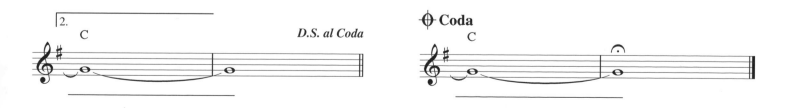

|2.

D.S. al Coda

⊕ **Coda**

Lord, You Have My Heart

Words and Music by Martin Smith

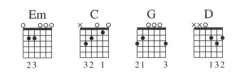

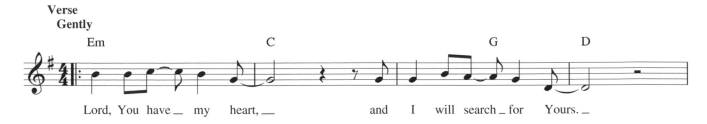

Verse
Gently

Lord, You have __ my heart, __ and I will search __ for Yours. __

Je - sus, take __ my life __ and lead me on.
Let me be __ to You __ a sac - ri - fice.

Chorus

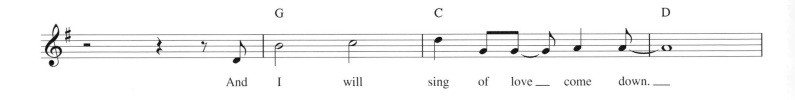

And I will praise You, __ Lord.

And I will sing of love __ come down. __

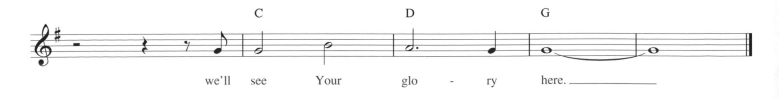

And as You show Your face,

we'll see Your glo - ry here. __

I Will Rise

Words and Music by Chris Tomlin, Jesse Reeves, Louie Giglio and Matt Maher

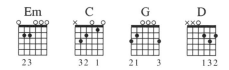

Verse
Gently

1. There's a peace I've come to know, though my
(2.) day that's draw - ing near, when this

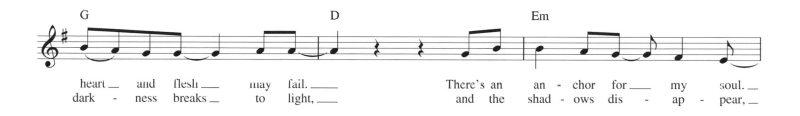

heart and flesh may fail. There's an an - chor for my soul.
dark - ness breaks to light, and the shad - ows dis - ap - pear,

I can say, "It is well." ⎬
and my faith shall be my eyes. ⎬ Je -

Pre-Chorus

- sus has o - ver - come, and the grave is o - ver - whelmed.

The vic - to - ry is won; He is

ris - en from _____ the dead. _____ And I _____ will rise ___

Chorus

____ when He calls ___ my name; ___ no ___ more sor - row, no ___

____ more pain. __ I will rise _____ on ea - gles' wings; _ be - fore _

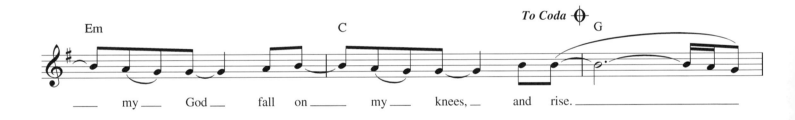

____ my ___ God ___ fall on ____ my ___ knees, __ and rise. _____

I will _ rise. _____ 2. There's a _____ And I hear the voice _

Bridge

____ of man - y an - gels sing, _ "Wor - thy is _____ the Lamb!" _

D   C   G   D

And I hear the cry ___ of ev - 'ry long - ing heart, _ "Wor -

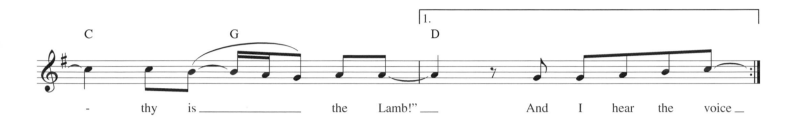

C   G   1.   D

- thy is ___ the Lamb!" ___ And I hear the voice _

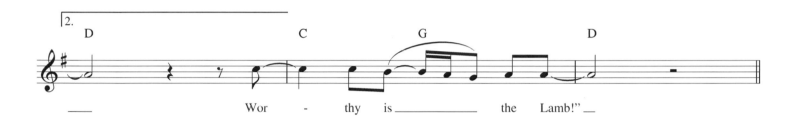

2.   D   C   G   D

___ Wor - thy is ___ the Lamb!" ___

Interlude   *D.S. al Coda*

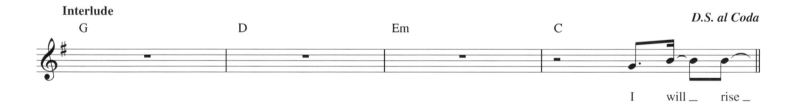

G   D   Em   C

I will _ rise _

Coda

G   C   G

I will _ rise. ___

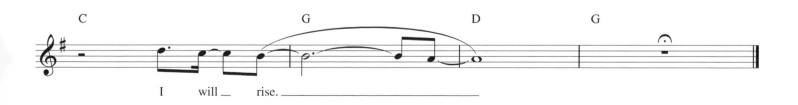

C   G   D   G

I will _ rise. ___

Love the Lord

Words and Music by Lincoln Brewster

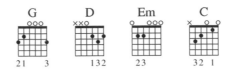

Intro
Moderately fast, in 2

Da, da, dum,   da, da, dum,   da, da, da. _____   Da, da, dum,

da, da, dum, da, da, da. _____   Da, da, dum,   oh, ____ yeah. ____

Verse

1. Love the Lord __ your God __ with all __ your heart, __ with all __ your soul, __ with all __ your mind, __
2. I will serve __ the Lord __ with all __ my heart, __ with all __ my soul, __ with all __ my mind, __
3. I will love __ You, Lord, __ with all __ my heart, __ with all __ my soul, __ with all __ my mind, __

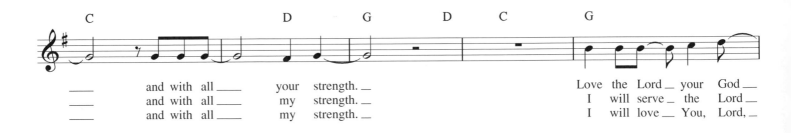

___ and with all ____ your strength. __   Love the Lord __ your God __
___ and with all ____ my strength. __   I will serve __ the Lord __
___ and with all ____ my strength. __   I will love __ You, Lord, __

___ with all __ your heart, __ with all __ your soul, __ with all __ your mind, __   and with all __
___ with all __ my heart, __ with all __ my soul, __ with all __ my mind, __   and with all __
___ with all __ my heart, __ with all __ my soul, __ with all __ my mind, __   and with all __

With all — my heart, — with all — my soul, — with all — my mind, —

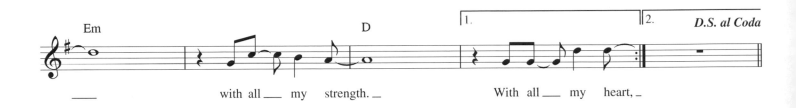

— with all — my strength. — With all — my heart, —

— I — will love You. Da, da, dum, da, da, dum, da, da, da. —

— Da, da, dum, da, da, dum, da, da, da. — Da, da, dum, oh, — yeah. —

I will love — You, Lord, — with all — my heart, — with all — my soul, —

*Let chords ring to end.

— with all — my mind, — and with all — my strength. —

Lord Most High

Words and Music by Don Harris and Gary Sadler

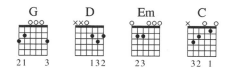

Verse
Moderately fast

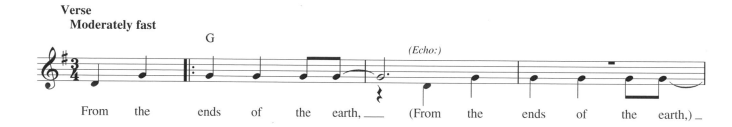

From the ends of the earth, ___ (From the ends of the earth,) ___

___ from the depths of the sea, ___ (from the depths of the sea,) ___

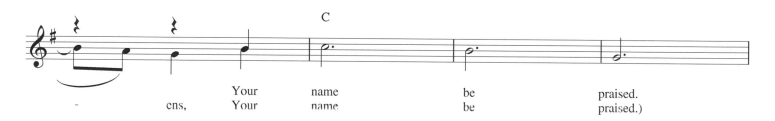

___ from the heights of the heav - ens, (from the heights of the heav -

ens, Your name name be be praised.
Your name be praised.)

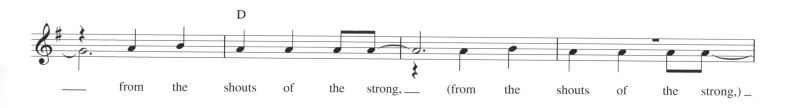

From the hearts of the weak, ___ (From the hearts of the weak,) ___

___ from the shouts of the strong, ___ (from the shouts of the strong,) ___

_____ from the lips of all _____ peo - ple, (from the lips of all _____

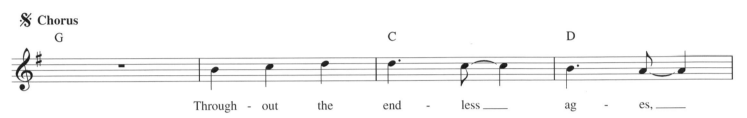

peo - ple, this song we raise, Lord.
_____ this song we raise, Lord.)

𝄋 **Chorus**

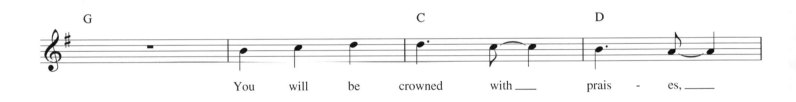

Through - out the end - less _____ ag - es, _____

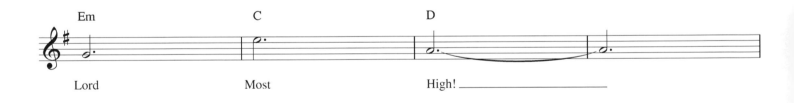

You will be crowned with _____ prais - es, _____

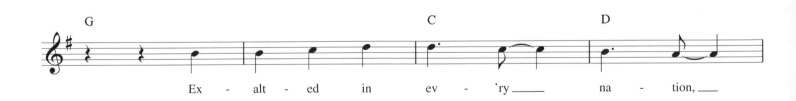

Lord Most High! _____

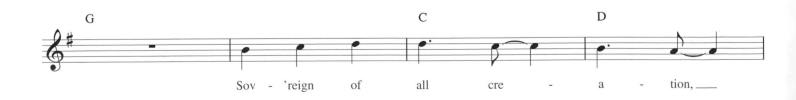

Ex - alt - ed in ev - 'ry _____ na - tion, _____

Sov - 'reign of all cre - a - tion, _____

Lord   Most   High,   be   mag - ni -

fied. _____   From   the

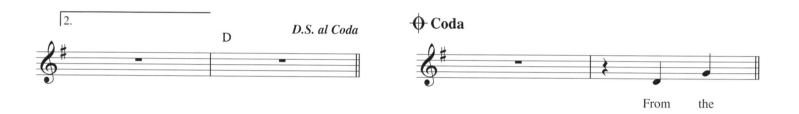

From   the

Outro-Verse

hearts   of   the   weak, ___ (From   the   hearts   of   the   weak,) ___   from   the

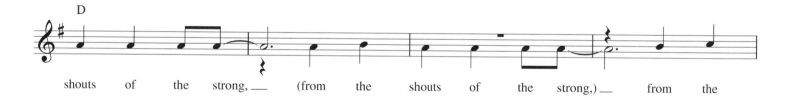

shouts   of   the   strong, ___ (from   the   shouts   of   the   strong,) ___   from   the

lips   of   all ___   peo - ple,   this
                    (from   the   lips   of   all ___   peo - ple,   this

song   we   raise... _____
song   we   raise...) _____

39

Mighty to Save

Words and Music by Ben Fielding and Reuben Morgan

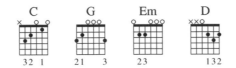

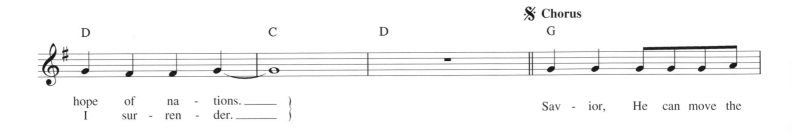

ev - er Au - thor of sal - va - tion, He rose and con - quered the grave, __ Je - sus

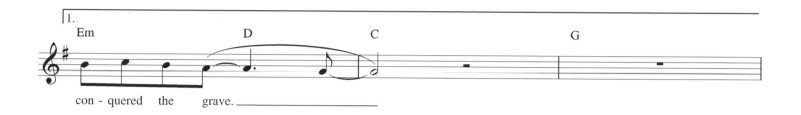

1.

con - quered the grave. _____

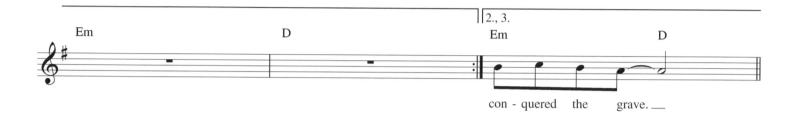

2., 3.

con - quered the grave. __

Bridge

Shine your light and ____ let the whole world ____ see we're sing - ing

for the glo - ry ____ of the ris - en ____ King, ____ Je - sus.

Shine your light and ____ let the whole world ____ see we're sing - ing

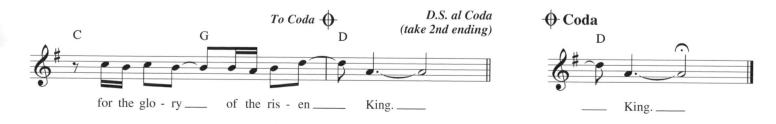

To Coda **D.S. al Coda** *(take 2nd ending)* **Coda**

for the glo - ry ____ of the ris - en ____ King. ____   ____ King. ____

No One Like You

Words and Music by Jack Parker, Mike Dodson, Jason Solley, Mike Hogan, Jeremy Bush and David Crowder

And how could I ev-er de-ny the love of my Sav-ior?

You are to me ev-'ry-thing, all I need for-ev-er.

Pre-Chorus

How could You be so good?

Chorus

There is no one like You.

There has nev-er ev-er been an-y-one___ like You.

Interlude

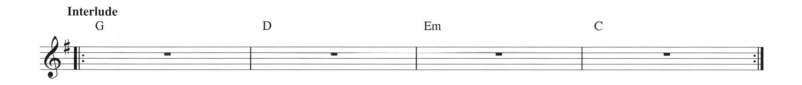

Verse

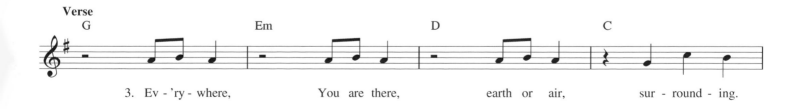

3. Ev-'ry-where, You are there, earth or air, sur-round-ing.

I'm not a - lone, the heav - ens sing a - long. My God, You're so

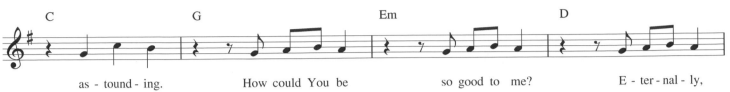

as - tound - ing. How could You be so good to me? E - ter - nal - ly,

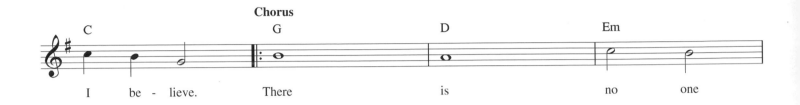

Chorus

I be - lieve. There is no one

like You. There has nev - er ev - er been

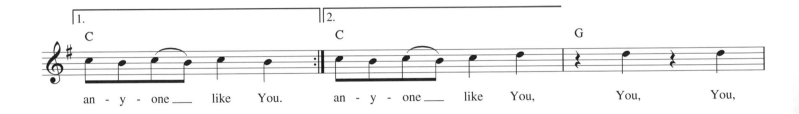

1.   2.

an - y - one ___ like You.   an - y - one ___ like You, You, You,

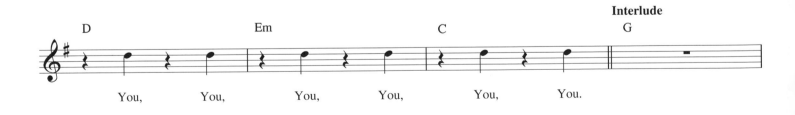

Interlude

You, You, You, You, You, You.

Bridge
Half-time feel

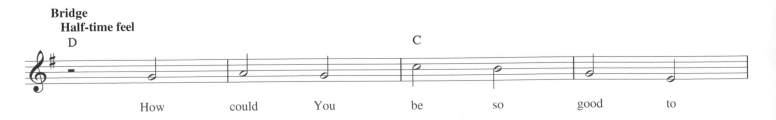

How could You be so good to

me? (How could You be so good to

me?) How could You be so good to

me? (How could You be so good to

me?) We're not a - lone, so sing a - long.

We're not a - lone, so sing a - long,

End half-time feel

N.C.

sing a - long, sing a - long.

Chorus

There is no one like You. There has

nev - er ev - er been an - y - one __ like You.

Shout to the North

Words and Music by Martin Smith

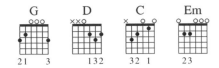

Verse
Moderately slow, in 2

1. Men of faith, rise up and sing of the great and glo - rious
   wom - en of the truth; stand and sing to bro - ken
   church with bro - ken wings; fill this place with songs a -

King. You are strong when you feel weak; in your bro - ken - ness, com -
hearts who can know the heal - ing pow'r of our awe - some King of
gain of our God who reigns on high. By His grace, a - gain we'll

Chorus

plete.
love.
fly.

Shout to the north and the south,

sing to the east and the west. Je - sus is Sav - ior to all,

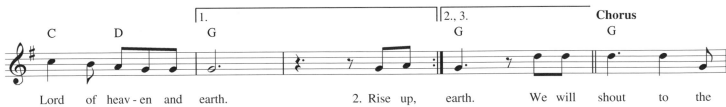

1. Lord of heav - en and earth.
2., 3. **Chorus** 2. Rise up, earth. We will shout to the

To Coda

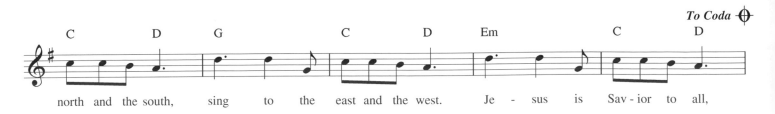

north and the south, sing to the east and the west. Je - sus is Sav - ior to all,

Lord of heav-en and earth.

Bridge

We've been through fire,___ we've been through rain.

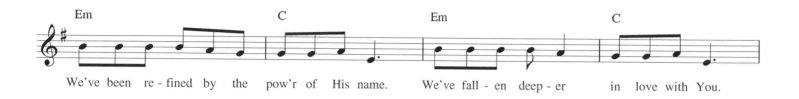

We've been re-fined by the pow'r of His name. We've fall-en deep-er in love with You.

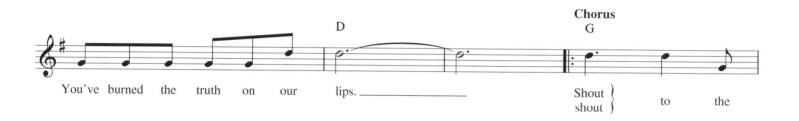

Chorus

You've burned the truth on our lips.___ Shout / shout to the

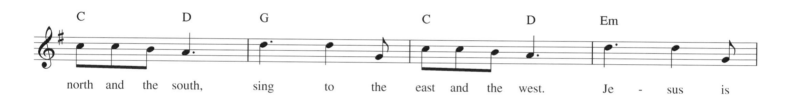

north and the south, sing to the east and the west. Je - sus is

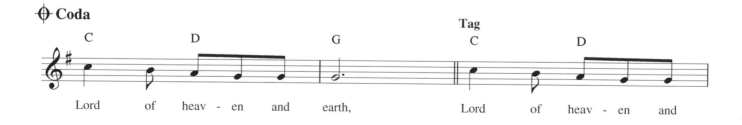

Sav-ior to all, Lord of heav-en and earth. We will earth. 3. Rise up,

Coda

Tag

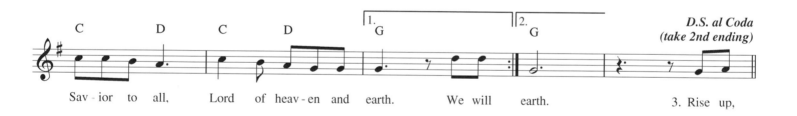

Lord of heav - en and earth, Lord of heav - en and

earth, oh,___ Lord of heav - en and earth.

Trading My Sorrows

Words and Music by Darrell Evans

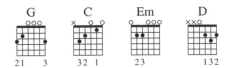

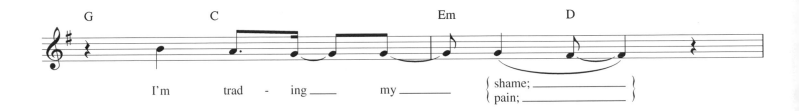

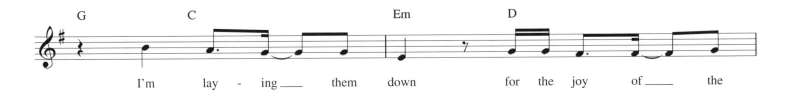

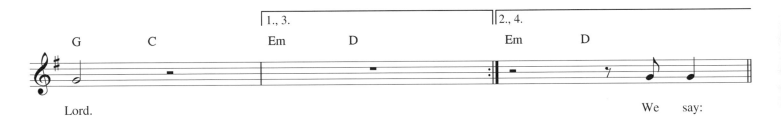

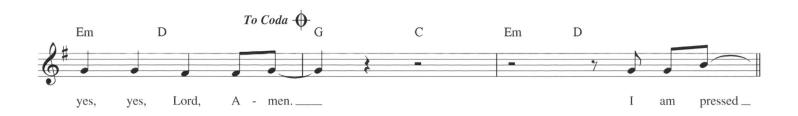

yes, yes, Lord, A - men. ____ I am pressed ____

Bridge

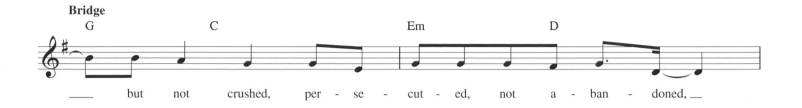

____ but not crushed, per - se - cut - ed, not a - ban - doned, ____

struck down ____ but not de - stroyed. I am blessed ____

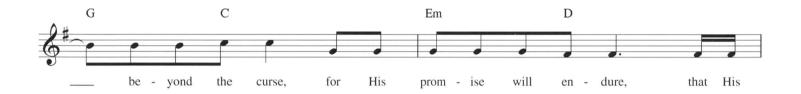

____ be - yond the curse, for His prom - ise will en - dure, that His

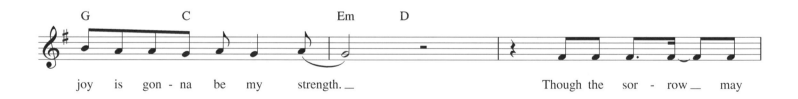

joy is gon - na be my strength. __ Though the sor - row __ may

last for ____ the night, His joy ____ comes with the morn -

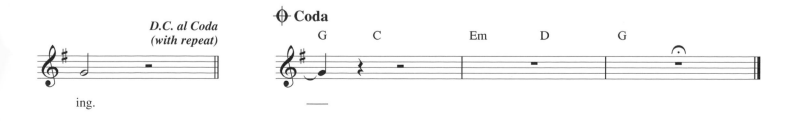

ing. ____

Unashamed Love

Words and Music by Lamont Hiebert

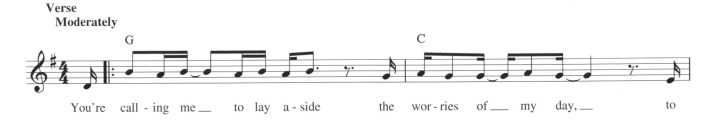

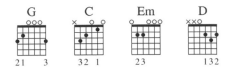

Verse
Moderately

You're call-ing me to lay a-side the wor-ries of my day, to

qui-et down my bus-y mind, find a hid-ing place.

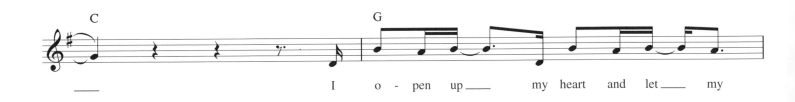

Wor - thy, You are wor - thy. I o - pen up my heart and let my

spir-it wor-ship Yours. I o - pen up my mouth and let a song

____ of praise __ come forth. Wor - thy, _____ You are

wor - thy _____ of a __ child - like faith and

Chorus

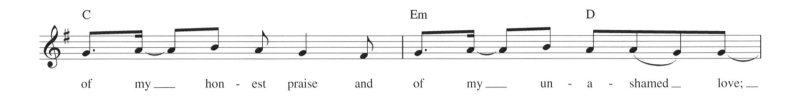

of my __ hon - est praise and of my __ un - a - shamed __ love; __

____ of a __ ho - ly life and of my __ sac - ri - fice and

of my __ un - a - shamed __ love. _____ You're

1.

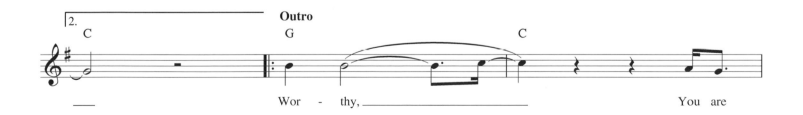

____ Wor - thy, _____ You are

2. **Outro**

wor - thy. _____

Unchanging

Words and Music by Chris Tomlin

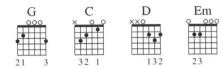

Verse
Moderately fast

1. Great is ___ Your faith - ful - ness, ___ great is ___ Your faith - ful - ness. ___

___ You nev - er change, ___ You nev - er fail, ___ O God. ___

Verse

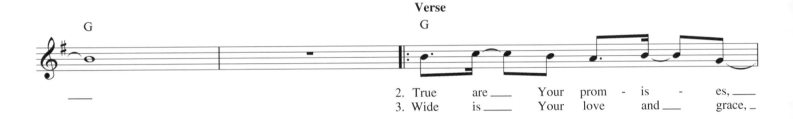

2. True are ___ Your prom - is - es, ___
3. Wide is ___ Your love and ___ grace, ___

true are ___ Your prom - is - es. ___ }
wide is ___ Your love and ___ grace. ___ }

You nev - er change, ___ You nev - er fail, ___ O God. ___

𝄋 Chorus

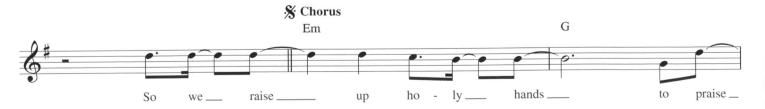

So we ___ raise ___ up ho - ly ___ hands ___ to praise ___

the Ho - ly One ____ who was _____ and is ___

___ and is ___ to come. ___ Yeah, we ___ raise ___ up ho - ly ___ hands ___

___ to praise ___ the Ho - ly One ____ who was ___

To Coda ⊕

_____ and is _____ and is ___ to come. ___

Bridge

You were, _ You are, ___ You will al - ways _ be. ____

You were, ___ You are, ___ You will al - ways ___ be. ___

D.S. al Coda ⊕ **Coda**

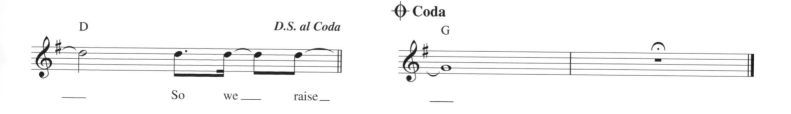

___ So we ___ raise _ ___

We Want to See Jesus Lifted High

Words and Music by Doug Horley

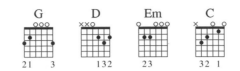

Verse
Fast

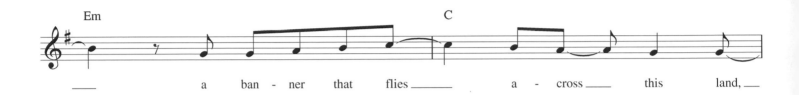

We want to see Je - sus lift - ed high,

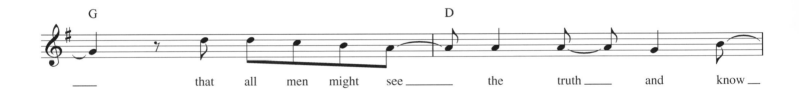

___ a ban - ner that flies ___ a - cross ___ this land, ___

___ that all men might see ___ the truth ___ and know ___

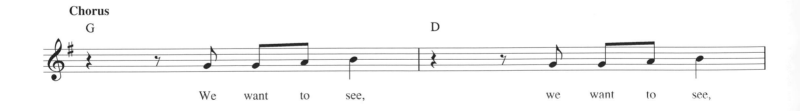

___ He is the way ___ to heav - en.

Chorus

We want to see, we want to see,

we want to see Je - sus lift - ed high.

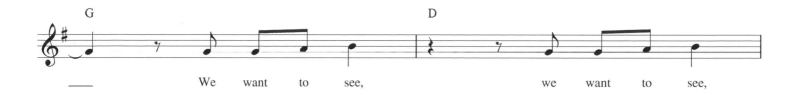

We want to see, we want to see,

we want to see Je - sus lift - ed high. ___

Bridge

___ Step by step we're mov - ing for -

- ward, lit - tle by lit - tle tak - ing ground. __

___ Ev - 'ry prayer _____ a pow'r - ful weap -

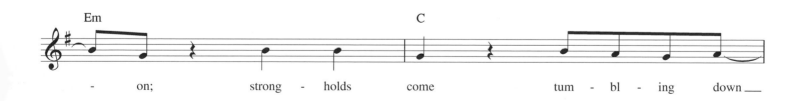

- on; strong - holds come tum - bl - ing down __

___ and down __ and down ___ and down. __   ___

christian guitar songbooks

from

ACOUSTIC GUITAR WORSHIP

30 praise song favorites arranged for guitar, including: Awesome God • Forever • I Could Sing of Your Love Forever • Lord, Reign in Me • Open the Eyes of My Heart • and more.
00699672 Solo Guitar...$14.99

FAVORITE HYMNS FOR SOLO GUITAR

Amazing Grace • Christ the Lord Is Risen Today • For the Beauty of the Earth • Holy, Holy, Holy • In the Garden • Let Us Break Bread Together • O for a Thousand Tongues to Sing • Were You There? • What a Friend We Have in Jesus • When I Survey the Wondrous Cross • more.
00699275 Fingerstyle Guitar $12.99

FINGERPICKING HYMNS

Abide with Me • Amazing Grace • Beneath the Cross of Jesus • Come, Thou Fount of Every Blessing • For the Beauty of the Earth • A Mighty Fortress Is Our God • Rock of Ages • and more.
00699688 Solo Guitar...$9.99

FINGERPICKING WORSHIP

Agnus Dei • Amazing Grace (My Chains Are Gone) • How Deep the Father's Love for Us • How Great Is Our God • I Worship You, Almighty God • More Precious Than Silver • There Is a Redeemer • We Fall Down • and more, plus an easy introduction to basic fingerstyle guitar.
00700554 Solo Guitar...$10.99

GOSPEL GUITAR SONGBOOK

Includes notes & tab for fingerpicking and Travis picking arrangements of 15 favorites: Amazing Grace • Blessed Assurance • Do Lord • I've Got Peace Like a River • Just a Closer Walk with Thee • O Happy Day • Precious Memories • Rock of Ages • Swing Low, Sweet Chariot • There Is Power in the Blood • When the Saints Go Marching In • and more!
00695372 Guitar with Notes & Tab $9.95

GOSPEL HYMNS

Amazing Grace • At the Cross • Blessed Assurance • Higher Ground • I've Got Peace like a River • In the Garden • Love Lifted Me • The Old Rugged Cross • Rock of Ages • What a Friend We Have in Jesus • When the Saints Go Marching In • Wondrous Love • and more.
00700463
Lyrics/Chord Symbols/Guitar Chord Diagrams........$14.99

HYMNS FOR CLASSICAL GUITAR

Amazing Grace • Be Thou My Vision • Come, Thou Fount of Every Blessing • For the Beauty of the Earth • Joyful, Joyful, We Adore Thee • My Faith Looks up to Thee • Rock of Ages • What a Friend We Have in Jesus • and more.
00701898 Solo Guitar...$14.99

HYMNS FOR SOLO JAZZ GUITAR

Book/Online Video

Abide with Me • Amazing Grace • Blessed Assurance • God Is So Good • Just a Closer Walk with Thee • Londonderry Air • Oh How I Love Jesus • Softly and Tenderly • Sweet Hour of Prayer • What a Friend We Have in Jesus.
00153842 Solo Guitar...$19.99

MODERN WORSHIP – GUITAR CHORD SONGBOOK

Amazed • Amazing Grace (My Chains Are Gone) • At the Cross • Beautiful One • Everlasting God • How Can I Keep from Singing • I Am Free • Let God Arise • Let My Words Be Few (I'll Stand in Awe of You) • Made to Worship • Mighty to Save • Nothing but the Blood • Offering • Sing to the King • Today Is the Day • Your Name • and more.
00701801
Lyrics/Chord Symbols/Guitar Chord Diagrams........$16.99

PRAISE & WORSHIP – STRUM & SING

This inspirational collection features 25 favorites for guitarists to strum and sing. Includes chords and lyrics for: Amazing Grace (My Chains Are Gone) • Cornerstone • Everlasting God • Forever • The Heart of Worship • How Great Is Our God • In Christ Alone • Mighty to Save • 10,000 Reasons (Bless the Lord) • This I Believe • We Fall Down • and more.
00152381 Guitar/Vocal...$12.99

SACRED SONGS FOR CLASSICAL GUITAR

Bind Us Together • El Shaddai • Here I Am, Lord • His Name Is Wonderful • How Great Thou Art • I Walked Today Where Jesus Walked • On Eagle's Wings • Thou Art Worthy • and more.
00702426 Guitar...$14.99

SUNDAY SOLOS FOR GUITAR

Great Is Thy Faithfulness • Here I Am to Worship • How Great Is Our God • Joyful, Joyful, We Adore Thee • There Is a Redeemer • We Fall Down • What a Friend We Have in Jesus • and more!
00703083 Guitar...$14.99

TOP CHRISTIAN HITS – STRUM & SING GUITAR

Good Good Father (Chris Tomlin) • Greater (MercyMe) • Holy Spirit (Francesca Battistelli) • I Am (Crowder) • Same Power (Jeremy Camp) • This Is Amazing Grace (Phil Wickham) • and more.
00156331 Guitar/Vocal...$12.99

THE WORSHIP GUITAR ANTHOLOGY – VOLUME 1

This collection contains melody, lyrics & chords for 100 contemporary favorites, such as: Beautiful One • Forever • Here I Am to Worship • Hosanna (Praise Is Rising) • How He Loves • In Christ Alone • Mighty to Save • Our God • Revelation Song • Your Grace Is Enough • and dozens more.
00101864 Melody/Lyrics/Chords..........................$16.99

WORSHIP SOLOS FOR FINGERSTYLE GUITAR

Ancient Words • Before the Throne of God Above • Broken Vessels (Amazing Grace) • Cornerstone • Good Good Father • Great Are You Lord • Holy Spirit • I Will Rise • King of My Heart • Lord, I Need You • O Come to the Altar • O Praise the Name (Anastasis) • Oceans (Where Feet May Fail) • 10,000 Reasons (Bless the Lord) • Your Name.
00276831 Guitar...$14.99

TOP WORSHIP SONGS FOR GUITAR

Amazing Grace (My Chains Are Gone) • Because He Lives, Amen • Cornerstone • Forever (We Sing Hallelujah) • Good Good Father • Holy Spirit • Jesus Messiah • Lead Me to the Cross • Our God • Revelation Song • This Is Amazing Grace • We Believe • Your Grace Is Enough • and more.
00160854 Melody/Lyrics/Chords..........................$12.99

Prices, contents and availability subject to change without notice.

FOR MORE INFORMATION,
SEE YOUR LOCAL MUSIC DEALER,
OR WRITE TO:

HAL•LEONARD®
7777 W. BLUEMOUND RD. P.O. BOX 13819
MILWAUKEE, WISCONSIN 53213

www.halleonard.com